my itty-bitty bio

Lionel Messi

Published in the United States of America by Cherry Lake Publishing
Ann Arbor, Michigan
www.cherrylakepublishing.com

Reading Adviser: Beth Walker Gambro, MS, Ed., Reading Consultant, Yorkville, IL
Illustrator: Leo Trinidad

Photo Credits: © Simon Mayer/Shutterstock, 5; © Alessio Ponti/Shutterstock, 7; © kravik93/Shutterstock, 9; © chairoij/Shutterstock, 11; © Fabideciria/Shutterstock, 13, 23; © Fabideciria/Shutterstock, 15; © Sportimage Ltd/Alamy Stock Photo, 17, 22; © Abaca Press / Alamy Stock Photo, 19; © dpa picture alliance/Alamy Stock Photo, 21

Copyright © 2026 by Cherry Lake Publishing
All rights reserved. No part of this book may be reproduced or utilized in any form or by any means without written permission from the publisher.

Cherry Lake Press is an imprint of Cherry Lake Publishing Group

Library of Congress Cataloging-in-Publication Data has been filed and is available at catalog.loc.gov.

Printed in the United States of America

table of contents

My Story 4

Timeline 22

Glossary 24

Index 24

About the author: When not writing, Dr. Virginia Loh-Hagan serves as the Executive Director for AANAPISI Affairs and the APIDA Center at San Diego State University. She is also the Co-Executive Director of The Asian American Education Project. She lives in San Diego with her very tall husband and very naughty dogs.

About the illustrator: Leo Trinidad is a *New York Times* bestselling comic book artist, illustrator, and animator from Costa Rica. For more than 12 years, he's been creating content for children's books and TV shows. Leo created the first animated series ever produced in Central America and founded Rocket Cartoons, one of the most successful animation studios in Latin America. He is also the 2018 winner of the Central American Graphic Novel contest.

my story

I was born in 1987. I am from Argentina.

I moved to Spain.

My grandmother loved soccer. She inspired me to play.

She died when I was 11.

Who inspires you?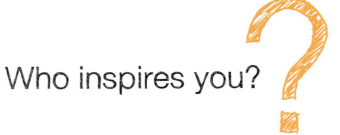

My brothers played.
My cousins played.

I played every day.

I was sick. My muscles and bones had a hard time growing.

I got help.

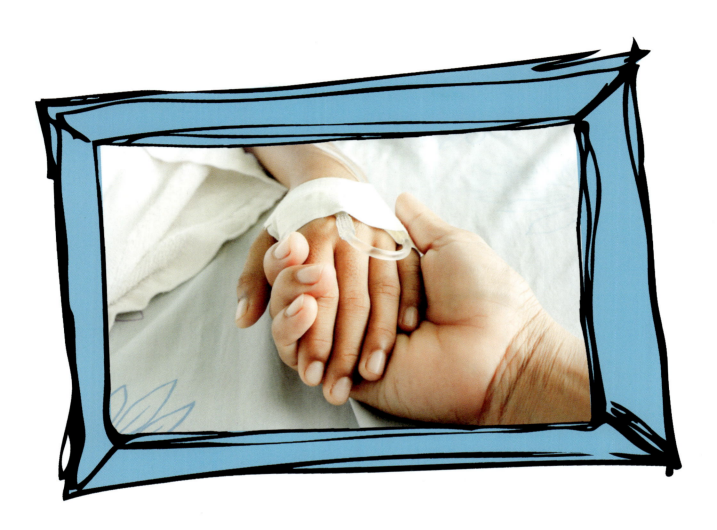

I play **professional** soccer. I won many games. I broke many records.

I won many awards.

Do you like to play sports?

I **dribble**. I pass. I weave through many players.

I know what I'm doing.

I score goals. I point to the sky.

I honor my grandmother.

I played in the **Olympics**.

I won a gold medal.

My legacy lives on.

I am one of the world's greatest soccer players.

What would you like to ask me?

timeline

2018

1970

Born
1987

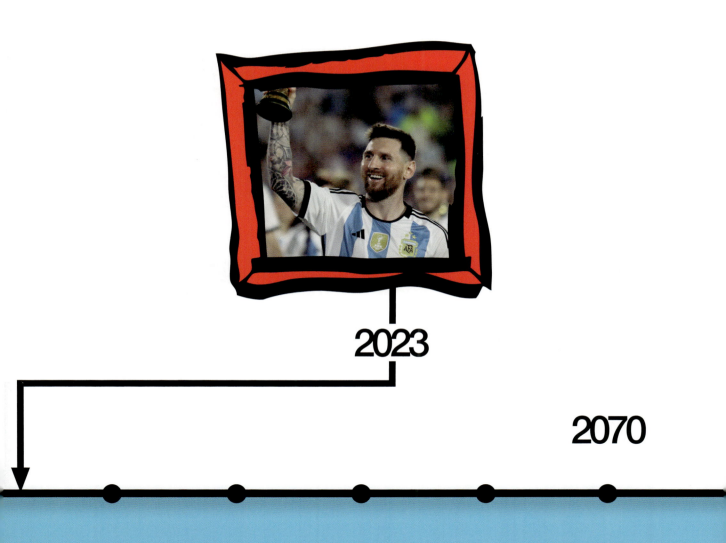

2023

2070

glossary & index

glossary

dribble (DRIH-buhl) to move the ball forward by kicking or tapping it back and forth

Olympics (uh-LIM-piks) international sports contests held every 4 years

professional (pruh-FESH-nuhl) related to a job; describing when someone is paid for their work

index

birth, 4, 22

family, 6, 8, 18

health, 10–11

Olympics, 18–19

professional career, 12–17, 20–21

soccer, 6–9, 12–21

talent, 12–18, 20

timeline, 22–23